D0532712

Colours
and Shapes

Meet Bip, Bop, and Boo!

Bip the Cat knows all about number problems.

Bip supports your child's numeracy and science learning.

Cuddly Bop the Elephant likes words and stories.

Bop helps your child's language development.

Boo the Monkey loves make-believe play and art.

Boo encourages your child's creative, physical, and social skills.

How to use this book

- Use this book together. Read the activities aloud to your child.

- Help your child take off the stickers and put them the right way up into the space.

- Always stop before your child becomes tired. Return to the page the next time.

- Give plenty of praise and encouragement as your child completes each activity.

- Look for any opportunities for asking questions about colours and shapes in your child's everyday experiences. Page 30 gives some examples.

DK | Penguin Random House

Senior Editor Deborah Lock
Senior Designer Victoria Harvey
Illustrator Reg Silva
Pre-production Editor
Andy Hilliard
Art Director Helen Senior
Educational Consultant
Penny Coltman

First published in Great Britain by
Dorling Kindersley Limited
80 Strand, London, WC2R 0RL
Copyright © 2015 Dorling
Kindersley Limited
A Penguin Random House
Company
10 9 8 7 6 5 4 3 2 1
001—271140—July/2015
All rights reserved.

Without limiting the rights under

A CIP catalogue record for this
book is available from the British
Library.
ISBN: 978-0-2411-8459-2

Printed and bound in China

The publisher wishes to thank
Atsuko Burnett for making Bip,
Bop, and Boo; Dawn Sirett for
editorial work. The publisher
would like to thank the following
for their kind permission to
reproduce their photographs:
(Key: a-above; b-below/bottom;
c-centre; f-far; l-left; r-right; t-top)
4 Dorling Kindersley: Andy
Woolley (ca). **Stickers: Alamy
Images:** ian nolan (bench).
Dorling Kindersley: Alfie Orkin
(white car).

All other images
© Dorling Kindersley
For further information see:
www.dkimages.com

A WORLD OF IDEAS:
SEE ALL THERE IS TO KNOW

www.dk.com

Contents

Red, blue and yellow

Beep! Beep! Brrrm! There are three garages: one red, one blue and one yellow.

Find the vehicle sticker for each garage. **Match** the vehicle colour to the garage colour.

Bop says, "Do you have any toy vehicles. What colours are they?"

Bip asks, "How many bikes can you see?"

Now **find** a butterfly sticker to put in the sky next to each garage. **Match** the butterfly colour to the garage colour.

Green, orange, purple and brown

What can you see in each painting?
Name the colours you can see.
Find the pots of paint stickers.
Place the right colour pot under each picture.

a green leaf

an orange fish

Boo says, "Draw your own picture in this frame."

a purple flower

a brown rabbit

7

Pink, white and black

Wow! Look at all the birthday presents.
Some are pink, some are white
and some are black.

Find the missing toy sticker for each
present box. Its colour matches its box.

Now **find** a bow sticker to put on each box.
Match the bow colour to the box.

Light and dark colours

Nature is full of colours.

Find the light green leaves sticker to put onto the light green tree.

Bop says, "Say the colours of the rainbow: red, orange, yellow, green, blue, violet and indigo."

Find the dark green leaves sticker to put onto the dark green tree.

Colour the flowers light blue and dark blue.

11

Pretty patterns

The clothes are drying on the washing line.
What pretty patterns can you see?

Find the sticker for the missing sock with a star pattern.

Bop says, "Name the colours on the stripy underwear."

What colours can you see on the flowery dress?

Find the sticker for the checked pyjama top.

Boo says, "I have a stripy pattern. Are you wearing any patterns on your clothes?"

Following lines

The fire engine is driving back to the fire station.

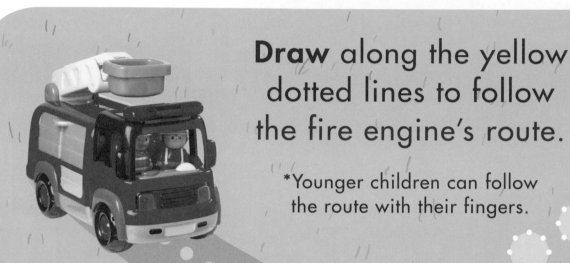

Draw along the yellow dotted lines to follow the fire engine's route.

*Younger children can follow the route with their fingers.

Put the daisy stickers around the roundabout.

Bop says, "What sound does a fire engine make?"

Boo asks, "Is my tail straight or curved?"

Point to the roads that curve.

Put the straight bench sticker next to the straight road.

15

Edges

Look at the shapes of the leaves.

Find the leaf sticker with a pointy edge.

Follow the spiky edge of the prickly holly leaf.

Which leaf has a zig-zag edge?

Boo asks, "What colours are the leaves?"

Find the leaf sticker with a wavy edge.

Round shapes

Teddy bear is having a picnic.

Point to the round-shaped plates on the picnic mat. **What** other round shapes can you see?

Bip says, "Which cake is the biggest?"

Find the round stickers for the buttons on the teddy bear's jumper.

Colour the teddy bear's badge. **What** shape is it?

A circle is a round shape.

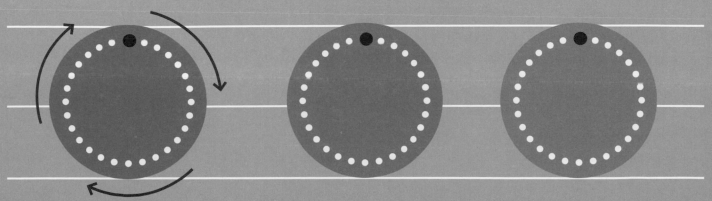

Follow the dots for the circle with your finger. Begin at the black dot and go all the way around. Try some more.

19

Triangles

It's time for tea.

The pizza has been cut into triangle shapes. **Count** the corners on each slice of pizza.

Put the 3 triangle napkin stickers on the tablecloth.

Bip says, "How many triangles are on Dolly's crown?"

Find the triangle stickers for Dolly's crown.

Colour Dolly's necklace and flag. **What** shape are they?

A triangle is a 3 sided shape with 3 corners.

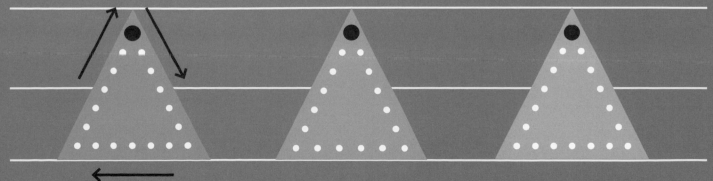

Follow the dots for the triangle with your finger. Begin at the black dot and follow the arrows. Try some more.

Rectangles

Look at the shapes of the objects on the desk.

Follow the dots with your finger around the 4 straight sides of the rubber, the piece of paper and the ruler. **Count** the corners on the pencil case.

Find the rectangle stickers to finish the robot picture.

Colour the rectangle ears on the robot.

Bop asks, "How many things can you think of that are shaped like a rectangle?"

A rectangle has 4 straight sides.

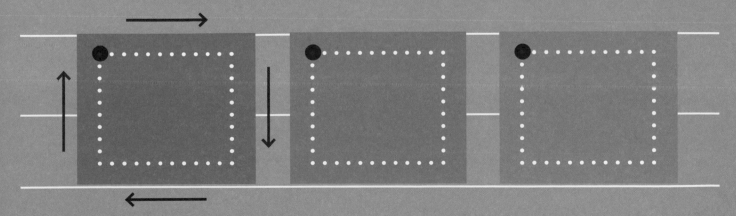

Follow the dots for the rectangle with your finger. Begin at the black dot and go straight along, down, along and up. Try some more.

Squares

Let's play with squares.

Here are some square-shaped cutters. **Match** their shapes to the play dough shapes. **Find** the smallest square.

Check that each square shape has 4 corners.

Bop says, "Name the colours of the play dough squares."

Here is a picture made of felt shapes.

Put the 2 square window stickers on the house.

Find the square plant pot sticker for the plant.

Boo says, "Can you see any square things around you?"

Squares are special rectangles.
All 4 straight sides are the same length.

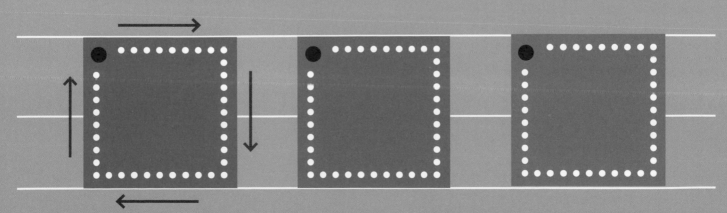

Follow the dots for the square with your finger. Begin at the black dot and go straight along, down, along and up. Try some more.

Stars and hearts

Look at the star and heart shapes on the dressing table.

Follow the dotted lines around the star and heart shapes. **Find** the heart-shaped sticker for the necklace.

Find 1 star sticker and 1 heart sticker to hang up with the other decorations.

Bip says, "How many points are on each star decoration?"

Star shapes have lots of points. Heart shapes have curves.

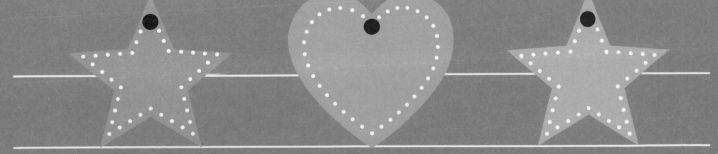

Follow the dots for the stars and heart with your finger. Begin at the black dots and follow the dotted lines around.

Colours, shapes and more!

What colours and shapes are on these pages?
Find the stickers for the missing shapes.

What patterns can you see?
Follow the wavy line of
the sea with your finger.

Boo says,
"Make your own
picture with
some shapes."

More activities to try!

Talk about the dark and light colours around you. **Find** different shades of the same colour.

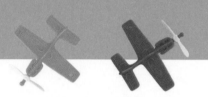

What colours and patterns are on your clothes today? **Talk** about what you will wear tomorrow.

Make a collection of different leaves. **How** are their shapes different? **Point** out the leaves with wavy edges, zig-zag edges, long or curved lines.

Press objects into dough or pastry to make different shapes. **Feel** around the edges. **Have** you made round or pointy shapes?

Well done!

You've finished Colours and Shapes

....

Write your name here.

From our Educational Consultant

DK always aims to offer content that prepares children for success in school and in life. In the DK **Get Ready for School** series, content is designed to address every aspect of a child's development, promoting important school-readiness skills such as critical thinking, creativity and communication.

The early years of a child's development really matter. As parents and carers, we must take every opportunity to encourage our children and inspire their enthusiasm for learning.

This series offers the opportunity for children to learn through familiar topics, discussion and playful activities. Children reach stages at different ages, so this series builds on past progress and guides children onto the next steps.

I am happy to partner DK as consultant on **Get Ready for School**. Life is a learning adventure, and you are your child's best teacher.

Penny Coltman,
Early Years Educational Consultant

. . . .

The three levels of the **Get Ready for School** Playbooks reinforce and support your child's development. Children reach developmental milestones at different rates but follow a similar progression of stages. The activities in the playbooks follow these learning stages to develop your child's confidence, curiosity and independence.

 Red Level 1 is for children who are beginning to make marks using a pencil, colouring and drawing; starting to recognise letters and numbers; beginning to develop the skills of counting and sorting; and showing interest in toys and the world around them.

 Yellow Level 2 is for children who are handling a pencil and scissors with increasing control; beginning to notice and recognise familiar words around them; matching numbers and quantity, and comparing objects; and using their experiences to imagine, construct, explore and question.

 Green Level 3 is for children who are bursting with growth in reading, writing, speaking and listening; looking closely at similarities, differences, patterns and change; beginning to apply adding and subtracting to solving problems; and constructing, imagining and experimenting with a purpose.

Pages 4 - 5

Pages 6 - 7

Pages 8 - 9